A Broken Heart Still Beats

L.V. Serrano

BookLeaf Publishing

India | USA | UK

Presentation by *BookLeaf Publishing*

Web: www.bookleafpub.com

E-mail: info@bookleafpub.com

ISBN: 9789363305038

First edition 2024

ACKNOWLEDGEMENT

First and foremost, I would like to thank God for everything. I would also like to thank my parents who had been supportive and loving throughout this whole process. I would like to thank my amazing family and spectacular friends, who are more like family at this point. I love each and every one of you dearly. I would also like to acknowledge you readers, thank you for taking a chance on this book. It touches my heart more than you'll ever know. Lastly, I would like to thank Bookleaf for this once in a lifetime and unforgettable experience! I will never get over this, and I want you all to truly know how grateful I am. In the wise words of the Miss Emily Dickinson, "For love is immortality".

Red Flags

It's confusing, I'd say
Because red means love and passion
But it also means danger and anger
So where do we draw the line?
When do we feel like we're giving up hope?
Or when we've hit our breaking point, take our
self-love first?
How do we decipher a small stop sign
From a whole red flag?
So we're supposed to stop
When we see red
But does love make us color blind?

Crashing

Blue crystal eyes
I have to get lost in them all over again
Waves crashing, drowning me under
The thought of me not being yours pulls me out
of the water though
My heart crashing for days
You misdelivered the cure
Heartbroken
Shattered
But you didn't try to stitch it back together
When you conveniently had the thread in your
hands
You weren't looking for me
While I already found you

Goodbye, Sun

Bright blonde hair like rays of sunshine
I used to joke we had a gravitational pull
Like the Earth to the Sun
The beginning was like the summer solstice, I
saw a lot of you
These days, however, the Sun sets earlier than
ever
Instead of being your sunflower, I was the plant
that always grew at an angle towards you
because I never got enough sunlight
It even got to the point where I could take my
sunglasses off
Because they weren't needed anymore
You're gone
Like the Sun, you were the center of my
universe. I wasn't yours, though
They say everything that goes up must come
down
Sunsets do indeed exist
So goodbye, Sun.

"Idk"

"Idk" was always your favorite response
But what made me confused was what I saw in
you for so long
Idk why I put up with you throwing away my
effort
Idk why I handpicked cute emojis for you
Idk why it took me so long to write this...
Because some part of me truly didn't want to let
you go
Some part needed time to process
To sum-up what made me conflicted
Idk why it took me this long
Idk what you didn't see in me
Idk why your heart didn't ache when I scraped
my knee
Idk why mine sank when you scraped yours
Idk why you never appreciated or cared
The biggest part, though, is that idk why I
wasted a whole poem on you
Maybe we both won't ever know.

Miss Overlooked

Do I ever cross your mind?
Like you cross mine
Date so many girls that aren't me
Can't you see?
I always like the boys who aren't single
But I'm always ready to mingle
Especially with you
What would it be like if we were together
We could just talk whenever
Wouldn't you at least like to try it?
My curse is that attractive boys are unavailable
Isn't it terrible?
Don't have Cupid shoot my heart just to break it
Because I've never faked it.

Waterloo

Every time I think I'm ready to move on
I think I can, but I still can't bring myself to play
that song
I knew hearing it would be the final straw
Even if I wanted you back, the last round was a
draw
It would be easier if we never met
If our paths decided to never intersect
I know you had a thing for me too
But I guess it was time for me to meet my
waterloo
So now I accept that you were a steppingstone, a
bridge to cross on
Don't you dare every look at me again with that
stare
Because one of the hardest things for me to do is
not care.

If Only This Was A Movie

I was too angry to cry
Too sad to scream
If this was a movie I wouldn't have stayed
If this was a TV show the season would be over
If this was a book everyone would write bad
reviews about your character
But this was real
I had to turn off the TV
Close the book
Because you were never mine
I had to stop writing plots you refused to follow
I had to let go of the little glimmer of hope
Forced to move on
So I don't know if you were the wrong person,
right time
And to you I was the right person, wrong time
All I know is that you were the best "hello"
And one of the worst "goodbye's".

Romeo

As I stood there, I watched you go
I couldn't stop you, I couldn't scream, that
would've been low
Cupid shot us both but at the wrong time
I say to tease us like that was a crime
Maybe one night I won't lay in bed
contemplating our "could've"
People say to let it go, I should've
But deep down I knew there was an "us"
Only in a world where time doesn't exist,
though, I put up a fuss
Part of me will never not care
Sadly life isn't fair
At least at one point I know we would've been
on the same team
Coach had to separate us, so now I will silently
cheer for you while you chase your dreams
For now I have to get over you
But you hold a key no one else holds, so if
circumstances change, we can hit "renew"
Wish there was a button labeled "reset"
But Romeo never did get Juliet.

Maybe One Day…

Either one day I'll forget you and all the gloom
Or I'll invite you to my wedding and kind of
wish you were the groom
No matter how many times I try to escape you
You always find a way to trap me back, how? I
have not a clue
They always say actions speak louder than
words
But what you did was turn "I like you too" into a
knife and stabbed me with it
Leaving me bleeding out, almost like an attack
I guess in the head we're all a little whack
But even my friends don't understand, what a
surprise
When we're together, though, I swear I see the
twinkle in your eyes
The fact that this hurts more than a break-up...
I beg you to take the hint
This proves how much I like you, I've been very
patient
So maybe one day I'll finally get over you
Or a part of me will forever be stuck under the
spell of you.

Gravestone

Honestly, it's your fault
When I told you how I felt, you said you felt the same
So why when the forecast was all sunny did all it do was rain?
I'm not a football but you fumbled me so hard
You picked me apart, ripped out my heart, and left me scarred
How are we the same age? You still act like a baby
I was about to settle for you, isn't that crazy?
To be clear, I didn't ask if you wanted to go to the whole moon with me
I was just curious if you wanted to stargaze, it would've been free
No one expected you on a knee
We were friends before so why can't we be friends after?
Did you think ignoring me would make it better?
You fell first
I fell harder
You fell too little
I fell too late
Now, no matter how painful, I must accept the fate

Even though you called me pretty on our first
date
I now am looking down at our gravestone slate.

It's Still Beating

"It's not that big of a deal"
"It's okay I guess"
"I'll get over it one day"
But what if that was all a lie?
I lost two people that day:
The boy I really liked
And a dear friend
The thing is, I didn't know which one hurt more
in the end
Did you know I go back everyday?
I play fine and act like it's all okay
What people don't know, though, is that I hope
to run into you again
We don't need to talk, you don't even need to
give me a head nod
I just need to see you...
Just
One
More
Time
I need my own pair of eyes to know you're alive
To know you weren't just all in my head
Would you have been a daydream or a
nightmare?

Is it possible that knowing you has been a
blessing and a curse?
Or now it's to have known you...
I believe this isn't where I'm supposed to write
"the end"
I know and hope our story doesn't end here
At this point, however, there isn't a cure
So I am living with a broken heart
But it's still beating, that's what's hard.

Glass

"She's glass" they always said
She was the aftermath
She hated her own reflection, so insecure
So she mirrored those around her instead
Glass doesn't really have bumps, it's close to
perfection
That's what she was
She watched the numbers on the scale decrease
But rise on the grade book
When light hits glass, it refracts into rainbows
That's what she was
She knew how to shine and turn it on only when
she was being observed under a spotlight
Glass is so easy to break
That's what she was
One critique completely crushed her, there went
her self worth
When there's shattered glass, we're taught to stay
away because it can hurt us
That's what she was
When she was broken on the inside, nobody
tried to glue her back
All they saw was the cuts she could give them,
but forgot about the beautiful vase she was
before they knocked her off the shelf

So she never took it as a compliment whenever someone whispered "she's glass".

Wind

Seasons change, like the phases of the moon
But wind was always the same
Blew down the leaves and spread pollen for the
bees
Wind cools a runner down on a jog
And makes the wishes of dandelion seeds waltz
in the air
Wind doesn't get the acknowledgment it
deserves
Just a shrug, maybe "oh that's just wind"
However, wind gets punished for spreading fires
in the forest
Then and only then does wind's presence get
addressed
Wind doesn't stop doing good, though
Wind still makes kites fly high in the sky
Wind carries the laughter of a child
But gets cursed for amplifying a baby's cry
So find your wind and hold them tight
Treat them right, for you they'd always fight.

Sweven

I don't cry, I write instead
I write to sort out all the unwanted thoughts in
my head
You're perfect on paper, you do everything right
So tell me why I have an internal fight
And I don't want to give you up
I don't want to hurt you like a toe stub
The devil on my shoulder keeps telling me
you're not him, and you'll never be
The angel tells me to let us be free
When we were together, do I wish I was there
with him?
The little voice in my head is real grim
My fear is that I'll get bored because things are
going well
That I'll be forced to utter "farewell"
My deeper fear is breaking your heart
Will this cause my whole world to fall apart?

Independence Day

If I could go back
I wouldn't regret anything
You were a really good "first"
We were a sunburst
We burned bright but too fast
When the fireworks were in the past
I had to face that we couldn't last
Thank you for all you did, and for not running
when I grilled you
I got lost in the corn maze of you, soon enough
though I had to run out
So from now on I declare my independence
But at least we had a peace treaty
So we had one last handshake
Then went our separate ways
I have nothing to say about you but praise.

Mending

The human heart is the strongest muscle in the
body
Mine weakens anytime I hear your name, so
really how well built is it?
How silly it is that our life depends on a tiny
organ that's so fragile and seems to always break
My heart was shattered and wanted a day off
But my brain told it to keep pumping
Every beat hurt but didn't destroy me
After the rain I knew always came the sun
For awhile I thought you were the only one
Then you shot me in the heart with a gun
I bled through the bandage I placed but didn't
completely bleed out
I think my blood will forever haunt you
Maybe your organ is a little broken too
So it's possible I'll see you again
Or this is it and we're forever done
Either way, my heart will mend itself.

I Wish

I wish I can scream stuff at you sometimes
But it's not fair, you're not to blame
I can't be mad at you, even though I am
Maybe I'm only mad because she isn't
You put her under a spell
You blinded her
Her contacts don't protect her anymore
Julia noticed it before Liv
Julia called for a crash cart
Liv was too stunned to do anything
She stood there, staring
Nurses scrambling
"Clear" Julia called
Thump, thump
Beep, beep, beeeeeep
Again
"Time of death, 1:02am" Julia called
"No..." Liv whispered
Liv ran into the room
Beeeeeeeeep
Liv started chest compressions
Beeeeeeeeep
Flatline
"Liv..." Julia called
But Liv didn't listen

Liv did chest compressions for almost half an
hour
Arm aching and all
"What happened?" Liv sobbed
"His heart stopped" Julia answered
Flatline
Click
Silence
"No. I wish..."
"I'm sorry"
Jack died
His heart kept beating
But not for her
That was the thing that hurt the most.

Circus

Circuses travel, like you do with girls
Bounce locations, stuck in the whirl
You're an entertainer, put on a good show
You tried to sell me on the idea of cotton candy,
but deep down I should've known it was too
sweet to be true
When the days were rainy, I always entered the
tent with a smile painted on my face
The lights and the shimmering costumes caught
my attention
So I was willing to watch every act
Tried my best to clap
I imperturbably waited for you to get on stage
and do a solo act
You did a few tricks but that was it
At the end of the day, a circus leader is a
performer
Does that mean it was all a lie?
All a joke
I went back but the circus was gone
The excitement over
The circus already moved on
I'll never see the show again
Even if I do
It won't be the old show
I'll never get the old version of you back.

Blur

We don't talk anymore
Not a wave
Can't even get a nod
I don't know what to say
If you think I went to see you, I didn't
You said we were good, but that's because you
can't handle conflict
We both knew the truth
In a perfect world I'd say "What happened to
you?"
What happened to the goofy and carefree boy
who stole my heart?
You had to get a haircut but for some reason
changed the inside too
It's like you're drowning in a world of blue
I don't know what happened to us
There technically wasn't even an "us"
But there was a friendship
A good one you demolished
I'll forever miss who you were
And the person you are now?
Is a complete question mark and a blur.

His P.O.V.

I'm sorry the fantasy you had in your head didn't
work out
I'm sorry the clouds covered the sparkling stars
When I see you, you seem fine
So maybe I never did matter that much to you
I can't tell you why but I had to make you slip
through my fingers
To be fair you didn't wave at me either
I have too much on my plate that losing you was
almost a relief
That still doesn't change the way I feel about
you, though
You would've just been another girl to dump me
soon enough
You used to believe I was the diamond in the
rough
After awhile you discovered that I don't shimmer
under every light
I was too overwhelmed to fight
You tried so hard to make me fit into your
puzzle
Tried every angle of my piece
I never fit in the conundrum
So it's sad seeing you
Knowing you were the right person
But never the right time.

Lighthouse

A tower that glows only at night
I put my full trust in it
We were enjoying the water, having a nice time
However the light never turned on...
We weren't warned
We crashed into land unexpectedly
Our boat broke, ruined
I thought we could fix it, I was willing to try
You thought it was too broken to repair
So we abandoned the boat
I was mad and false blaming the lighthouse for
never warning us
In reality, land was always there
We would've hit it eventually
We just hit it hard and fast and not soft and
expected
We lost our captain
The trip wore you out
So we didn't even really say "goodbye"
You just parted your separate way like I did
mine
Just know that if you ever choose to call, I'd pick
up
If you ever walk past me, I'd let you be

I would be more decent to you than you ever
were to me
Don't really know why
Part of me still is clinging to the old you
And refusing to accept this chance
The other part is sympathizing what you're going
through
You were my sailing partner after all, even for a
short time
That has to count for something, right?
Life always goes on
If our paths cross again, I'm willing to hear you
out
If not, a broken heart still beats.